IN THE SILENCE

Sister Char,

May God Bless You

He is an Eph 3:20

God!

Sherry Hill

How to attain true peace & self-discovery through the Lord's purpose

IN THE SILENCE

SHERRY HILL

TATE PUBLISHING & *Enterprises*

Published by Tate Publishing & Enterprises, LLC
127 E. Trade Center Terrace | Mustang, Oklahoma 73064 USA
1.888.361.9473 | www.tatepublishing.com

Tate Publishing is committed to excellence in the publishing industry. The company reflects the philosophy established by the founders, based on Psalm 68:11,
"The Lord gave the word and great was the company of those who published it."

Cover design by Amber Gulilat
Interior design by Chelsea Womble

Published in the United States of America

ISBN: 978-1-61739-533-8
1. Religion, Christian Life, Personal Growth
2. Religion, Christian Life, Inspirational
11.04.19

DEDICATION

To my mom, Jeanne,
for all that you are and what I aspire to be.
Thanks, Mom.

CHAPTER I

Silence
The silence is awakening
And it opens my heart
I started it and I want it to be complete
Silence is all around me
And it is my joy in life.
I feel like I'm awakening for the first time
I feel like my mouth is singing
Songs of praise
I desire to move into this new
And exciting realm
Oh God, please help me
To never lose this newness
Time is here
It will lead me to the truth

Silence is really all about truth. It's taking time to listen to your self and to listen to others.

When we do this, insight comes to us. This insight can be a profound experience, but it doesn't come overnight, it only comes with patience and discipline. How do we seek to acquire this insight? One way is we start to really listen. Did you hear me? I said really listen.

We have to listen to ourselves. The Self is our innermost being, and it beckons to us.

But the Self is quiet, and will only prompt us. It will never force or coerce. It is gentle and shy and will only come out when we ourselves are gentle and shy. Think of the times when you yourself have been in this quiet mood. I see this in myself when I'm reading. When we read a good book our emotions settle down. We start to concentrate and listen to what we are reading, especially if it's something that is teaching us how to cope with our ever demanding world.

Because for many of us, the world has beat on us for so long, that even though we are alive and breathing everything else is dead all around us. We need the life and Spirit of God to come and dwell in us. And the Spirit of God only comes through quietly seeking Him and displaying an attitude of humility. When we get serious with God, many times it's because we have come to the end of ourselves, and we realize we can't do it alone. Because what we have been doing has not made us happy, and it never will. God is there to pick us up, to renew and refresh us and to get us back on the right track. That's what we want, right? To get on the right path.

Some of you are on a path, but if you look around, you know it's not the right path.

Only God can satisfy. Only God can lead and direct us to the truth. The false self comes in and lies to us. It says, if you do this, you will be happy. So off we run and all we do is wear ourselves out. We have no joy, only a striving after the wind. Who can catch the wind? We sure can't, but I tell you God can. God is the Creator and finisher of all things.

We limit God when we only see Him in one area. You will never be happy until you surrender, and lay it down to Him. So why not start today?

When I first started this discipline, I took one thing at a time. I knew there were many areas that were wrong, but I also knew I didn't have to kill myself. God will show you one thing and you will start working on that. Then when you get some victory, He will show you something else, and on and on. We lose it because we jump ahead of God. We say, "Well, I have this wrong and this wrong and something else." And we start working on ten things and we're spiritually dying because we can't do it all at once. What you need to do, is stop, back up, and listen.

If we're not listening, how can we hear? We can't. We're so consumed with doing that everything else gets blocked out. We're running at a full sprint, and we're going to run out of energy and desire, and be so weak that we're not going to want to get up anymore. We need to slow down, listen to ourselves, listen to God, and let Him lead.

How do we listen? Let me give you an example: you're driving down the road, and the Self says to stop at this person's house, but our mind says, "I'm too busy and I'm tired." We're not listening and we're not being truthful with ourselves. The Self, our innermost being, knows what makes us happy. But we think what makes us happiest is going home and vegging. Wrong! This makes us miserable, because where not listening. Here comes in discipline. When the Self speaks, we need to slow down and listen, and when thoughts of fatigue come up, which are really the Me, say, "No, I'm doing something for myself." Now, should we never listen to the Me? No, of course not; we need balance, but many times we do nothing while the Self is screaming at us to move. We need to realize that too many times we listen to the Me, and the Me can never make us happy. It is only the Self that can.

Another way we truly listen is to ask ourselves, "What truly makes me happy?" Some of you are saying, "I don't know, whatever I'm doing it hasn't made me happy."

Have you ever known someone, maybe it's you, who previously did an activity, and then when you see them, they say, "You know, I haven't done that in years"? This is a clue.

Why do we give up the things we love? Because we think, I'm too old, I'm too busy, I have kids now. And the list could go on and on. What has happened? We've given up the Self and exchanged it for this worn out, overworked, too busy, too stressed individual, who is really a ghost of our true Selves. The Me will always go for more money, more position, more stress.

The Me never counts the cost, but the true self weighs everything.

What is the cost to new mothers that would love to stay at home with their newborn babies, but because of the new house, the two new car loans, and the designer clothes, they sacrifice the Self, and put their babies into daycare, feeling guilty and depressed and miserable. These women totally fall into, "I'd love to, but I can't," and I ask why? Can you get a part-time job? Can you refinance? Can you get rid of one new car, and get a cheaper second car? Can you buy nice clothes but at a cheaper department store? All these solutions are viable alternatives.

But the Me totally takes over, and you go right along down the path of misery. And if you would listen to the Self the Self is screaming at you, "You have options." But we never listen to the Self. The Self is pushed in the corner, and we ask ourselves later, "Why am I so unhappy?" Well? because you're not listening. Now as I said before, it doesn't happen overnight, we take it one step at a time.

How do we do that? We study. We seek out a plan. We implement our plan.

And our time frame? That depends on you. Some will move through this very quickly and make a decision and go with it. Others will take longer. But no matter how long it takes, don't skip the steps. If we skip the steps we may rush into an avenue that could be disastrous.

First we study; we look to see what the best path is for us. We seek out a plan to accomplish what we want and that will lead us to our dreams and desires. We implement our plan. With all these steps we take our time, we listen to God, as we apply it to our own individual situation. If you know you have to make your house payment and your car payment, you don't quit your job tomorrow unless you have total confirmation from God. Knowing then it's God doing it and not you, but in realizing that , God is a God of timing, and doing the steps gives God the time to work for you. To open up the doorways, for you to get what you want.

Here's an example from my own life. I hated my job, but I knew God had me there for a reason, and when God got ready, then God and only God would release me. And When He did release me I still had enough money to pay my bills and survive for an entire month, until He opened up another job for me. (But I did all the God steps; I didn't rush out ahead of God.

I applied the steps of listening, seeking and studying and implementing the best plan for me. I waited, even when I felt like screaming, because God was doing a work through me. And then after that God said, "We're done here, and we're moving on now."

And when God gets ready to move you, He'll move you.

Let's talk a little bit about moving, moving from one place to another, moving from one job to another, moving from one income bracket to another. We all want these things, we all desire them, and God wants to give them to you. So why isn't it happening? One reason is because of timing. Not our timing, but God's. Maybe that new place for you to live isn't available yet. Maybe the new job doesn't exist, and if God gave you more money now, all you would be is carnal with it. God knows us inside and out. He knows us better than we know ourselves. Really all we know is what the Me wants, we don't know ourselves. But as we continue to get more experienced, and more knowledgeable, and start seeking out the Self; and God, then when the time is right, nothing on earth or in hell can keep us from the blessings of God.

Sometimes other people can stop us from moving into the dream and destiny God has ordained for us. If we are hanging on to another individual too tightly they could hinder our walk with God and His advancement for us. Let me tell you, God doesn't care what's second, third, or even tenth in your life as long as He is always first. But if God is first then what is second, third, or tenth, He will always come along and modify.

God wants to be in total control. It's not about us anymore, and not us running to others, but us always running to Him first. When we run to God first it honors Him, and shows Him how much we truly love and trust Him.

And is it easy? No, it's not easy, but it is discipline. It's striving time after time to seek God out. To go to the Word, and see what it is He is trying to tell us. It's going to prayer, and when we're hurting and angry, and lonely, we go to Him our God and place it all before Him.

Because we are so weak, we can never do it alone. He has to help us and do a lot of it for us. And that doesn't mean casting your responsibility, but it does mean casting your cares upon Him.

> Casting the whole of your care [all your anxieties, all your worries, all your concerns, once and for all] on Him, for He cares for you affectionately and cares about you watchfully.
>
> 1 Peter 5:7 (Amplified Bible)

CHAPTER II

Silence is the key to the heart.
For it is in silence that we know ourselves.

To get quiet is truly our key to unlocking the Self. The Self is never pushy or forceful, that's the job of the Me. The Me gets us up in the morning, gets us going. We need the Me. But to find our true happiness, our worth and identity, we have to seek out the Self. And because the Self has been pushed around by the Me so much, the Self has really gotten shy. The Self will only come out in a quiet, peaceful, nurturing environment.

One of my favorite times for quiet, is in the morning. Mornings are when we are refreshed and renewed. I know what you're saying. "Mornings are crazy at my house." Possibly, getting up half an hour earlier would help you to have that quiet time. Or when you're alone in your car, turn off the radio and use that time to be quiet. We have many opportunities in our day to be quiet, what we are lacking is the mindset of using those opportunities. I'm sure many of you can think of times right now when you could have that quiet time. Be aware; when you start this discipline, the flesh will fight against it. But do it anyway, and don't let the devil steal from you your times of silence because he will if you are not extremely careful.

How? You get in your car, and your idea is not to have the radio on, but before you can turn it off, a good song comes on. Right away you need to say, "I've heard this song a million times I can miss it once," and, "God I believe, that because of this new discipline, later when I do want to listen to the radio, this song will come on again." Do you see the little steps of discipline? I'm not asking you to do some great thing, which totally would be a struggle for you. I'm asking you to look at yourself, and to see small areas that you can start using, to develop the Self. When you start to seek out the Self, you will start to discover hidden treasures.

What are these treasures? They are the areas in your life that have been covered up, by other people's influences, by not having your own priorities, or management of your own time. Let me give you an example,

I have a friend who hates loud music, but her husband loves it. And to make him happy she will force herself to sit there and listen to it with him when she could be engaging in a more rewarding activity that nourishes her soul. At the same time, he hates for her to do her meditation, and so because of his dislike she has discontinued to meditate.

What has happened here? A person has come into her life and has totally taken a part of her away, and now, she is existing as a shadow of her true self. She still exists but she's not complete. Parts of her identity are missing and she can't give fully to him or herself because she doesn't have fully to give. What we don't understand is when we give up activities that we love, we're actually giving up parts of ourselves. If we would look at it as giving up an arm or leg, right away we think, "No, I need that!"

But we have to see all these others as being just as vital to us. And that's what we miss. I know what some of you are thinking, "I can't do that activity all the time." Who's to say that you have to? I have found with myself that I like to jog. I don't do it all the time, but during different seasons of the year that desire will rise up within me, and I'll find I'll start jogging again. And I don't make it hard on myself by saying, "You worthless, lazy person you should be jogging." I just say, "Oh that will come around again." And I haven't eliminated it from my life because I really do like to jog, but it's not a burden. We have to be so careful about making things burdens, because a burden is one of the fastest things that will steal our joy and happiness.

So come on, be light on yourself, and take all these instructions seriously. Don't procrastinate or let the devil defeat you. See what you can do today, and start doing it.

CHAPTER III

Today is key.

Don't procrastinate, and don't delay. We need to actively pursue this new discipline. Because I'm telling you, the enemy will come in and distract you. If he can, he'll make you lose your determination, or he'll cause a storm in your life that will get you off track. How do we defeat the enemy? We don't delay; we engage, and we go forward.

> Eagerly pursue, and seek to acquire [this] love [make it your aim, your great quest]; and earnestly desire and cultivate the spiritual endowments (gifts)...
>
> Corinthians 14:1 (Amplified Bible)

That's really what it is; it's a quest, a quest for more fulfillment in our lives. More love, more peace, more happiness, and more joy. And how do we acquire these? We seek out our true selves and our true God. There are many gods out there, but the true God manifests Himself totally through us.

We serve a God who is not offended when we ask Him to reveal Himself to us. He is waiting and longing to be God in your life. But He will only do it if you ask Him to. God is a gentleman. He's not a bully standing up in heaven who wants to hit you over the head. He wants to forgive you of your sins and to cast them as far as the East is from the West. He wants to love you, and nurture you, and hold you. He wants to be your father, your mother, your friend, your confidant, your God.

Please open your heart today and let Him come in? He stands at the door and knocks but only you can open it. And if all you can do today is open it a crack, then He will accept that. Remember; take it one step and one day at a time. Don't rush, don't force. Be easy, be light, and be gentle.

> "For My yoke is wholesome (useful, good-not harsh, hard, sharp, or pressing, but comfortable, gracious, and pleasant), and My burden is light and easy to be borne.
>
> Take My yoke upon you and learn of Me, for I am gentle (meek) and humble (lowly) in heart, and you will find rest, (relief and ease and refreshment and recreation and blessed quiet) for your souls."
>
> Matthew 11:30 and 29 (Amplified Bible)

God is never harsh. We are the ones who are harsh. We are the ones beating ourselves over the head. The Me in God is perfect, but the Me in us is selfish, controlling, and sinful. And because of that sinfulness, our God is put at a distance. What we have to do is humble ourselves, and push out the Me so that the Me in God can work in us to bring us to a new awareness of ourselves.

And as we allow God to come in and take over more and more, then what happens is we start taking on the attributes of our God. And He instills in us worth, holiness, purification, and the fruits of the Spirit. What are these fruits?

> But the fruit of the [Holy] Spirit [the work which His presence within accomplishes] is love, joy, (gladness), peace, patience (an even temper, forbearance), kindness, goodness, (benevolence), faithfulness, gentleness (meekness, humility), self-control (self-restraint, continence). Against such things there is no law [that can bring a charge].
>
> Galatians 5:22–23 (Amplified Bible)

All these fruits take time, even years. But what do you have to lose? Oh you lose misery, unhappiness, nervousness, sinfulness. And you gain joy, peace, love, patience, a wholesome mind and a wholesome spirit. Is it easy? No! It takes discipline.

Look at a college student. That first summer before they even start classes, they're excited. New adventures are ready to unfold in their lives, new friends, and a new atmosphere. But along with that comes hard work and many don't make it through. Why? Because they either don't do the work and flunk out, or they quit in the middle.

We have to be a people, who don't quit. Set your mind and keep it set. Don't lose the vision. And how many times have you gone back to those who didn't make it? And what do they say? "If only I'd done this." We'll good news, today's a new day. I was one of those people who quit. But today, ten years later, I'm going back. And I am so excited. I never lost the vision. It was dormant, but one thing I always said, "I can go back. It is only me stopping myself." Don't live your life letting the Me stop you.

What have you quit? What have you lost? It's still available for you. It hasn't gone anywhere. Pick it up, trust in God and He will lead you back to yourself. It's the things that we give up and quit, that steal the life from us. ,Satan wants us to live this lazy, pathetic, do-nothing life. God has placed a spirit of can do in us.

But when we lose God, we lose our hope; we lose our vision, and then stand around wondering why we are so miserable and depressed. We have fallen into the pit of despair and worthlessness. But God is standing on the edge with His hand ready, to lift us out. But what we always see is the enemy on the other side, saying, "You're nobody," "You can't do anything," "You're lazy," or, "You're stupid."

And we stay in the pit believing the lies. The Me gets stronger and the Self gets weaker and weaker because we believe the Me lies. But I tell you today, there is a God. That if you reach out, His power will infuse you and lift you totally and completely out of that pit. But your job is to reach out. Lift up your hand today and reach out. He's waiting and will continue to wait. He won't leave you. He loves you so much. Take His hand today. Reach out and come into a new and glorious life and future. Come into your destiny and see what God will do for you. He's waiting; don't delay. Right now is the time, the hour, the day. Cast off your depression and doubt, and let God be God.

CHAPTER IV

In the silence of destiny
Everywhere she could feel the air
It touched her arm
And blew though her hair
She had beautiful hair long and black
She kept it bound for she was fair
She was fair of body and of soul
A soul that could encompass all her dreams
And so every day she dreamed
To get from here to there
In a world of deceit and of lies
She rises above to see the sky
And in the clouds of her day
She sees the hand that leads the way

We really do all have a destiny. But if we're not tuned in to ourselves, we can go an entire lifetime and miss our destiny. This is one of the saddest things that happens in our world. So many of us give up ourselves, and live this unhappy, lonely life, never realizing why.

The spouse's dream was not our dream. The kid's dream was not our dream. Our parents' dream was not our dream. But a lot of us go through life trying to live up to someone else's expectations and dreams. It's not in us to do. But we never realize that, and so we push ahead, trying to do this other dream, and then ask ourselves why we are so miserable. Once again it's the Me, the Me loves to be the martyr. The Me will sacrifice everything just to get that prideful feeling, "Oh I'm so wonderful, look at what I did." It's not a part of the true Self, it has nothing to do with our destiny, and God abhors this. And we're thinking, "God must be so proud of me, because I've sacrificed." We see this many times in a person's career choice. Why do we allow others to dictate to us what kind of job is best for us, is more appropriate or more successful. Don't allow this to happen to you.

> Has the Lord as great a delight in burnt offerings and sacrifices, as in obeying the voice of the Lord? Behold, to obey is better than sacrifice, and to hearken than the fat of rams.
>
> 1 Samuel 15:22 (Amplified Bible)

And, what are we supposed to hearken to? To the true Self. This is who we are, this is who God has made us to be. But the devil comes in with a lie and with the Me, and gets us totally off track. And that's where we become out of balance, and we are miserable.

God is not a God of misery. He is a God who wants to bless His obedient children and to lead them to truth. And that is where the Self is the ruler and umpire of the flesh. The flesh is full of pride, full of sacrifice, and full of doing it our own way. On the other hand, the Self is full of quietness, truth, and seeking to do it the right way. Let's say that right now, many of you are thinking, "Okay, I get this, but where do I start to discover my true Self?"

One way you can start is your style. Look around your house, and ask yourself, "What do I like?" Some of you will have instruments that are sitting there and getting dusty from lack of use. These aren't big things that are telling you to quit your job and change your life. For many of you this will be an addition to your life, making it richer and fuller. Another way is prayer. Maybe God had a vision and dream for you in ministry, but because you got off track, you forgot all about this calling of God.

And let me tell you, it is never too late to get back on track with God. God is so wonderful. He can still use us. And we all want to be used by God. But it is only the true Self that knows the path. The Me comes to a fork in the road and says, "Let's go this way." Wrong. Stop. Ask the Self.

The Self will lead you through a cave, up a steep mountain pass, down into a barren desert. But if you go that way and trust the Self even though it's hard, even though the Me is screaming every step of the way, in the end the path will lead you to a glorious future. If you take the wrong path, oh it'll be easier. But in the end it will be like dust in your mouth. Nothing will ever come of it, misery will follow you, and the Self will always be with you, silently tugging at your heart. Go this way. Go this way. Go this way. I have seen this in my own life, when I allow the Self to emerge. In the beginning it was very hard, I felt like my whole world had turned upside down, but always when I would stick with my true desire it would lead me to the greater reward than if I had taken a more convenient route.

If we allow ourselves to take the convenient route the Self will get quieter and quieter, until it's just an uncomfortable prick in your heart. You'll go through life never realizing your true destiny and your true worth, because that's really what it's all about; your worth. We are a people who have lost our true worth.

We have women who don't know their true worth.

We have men who think their worth is only because of this job, or this activity. Our worth always comes back to the true Self, and the Self always leads us to God.

There are so many people who work a job because it's more money, but they hate the job. Why? Because the Me has gotten wrapped up in the money, and money can never make us happy, it makes us miserable. But the Me. It's always there lying to you, and we go right along believing. We have to question the Me beliefs. Don't believe everything the Me say's. It will lie to you and lead you down the wrong path. And then, at the end of our life we're saying, "I wish I could have. I wish I would have. I wish, I wish, I wish."

Well you can do that today. We do have the ability to change. We are a changing people. Our world is changing, our bodies are changing, and our minds are changing.

But now it's our job to take control of that change and use it for our own benefit. We need to control it ourselves. Don't allow it to control you. That's what many of us are doing right now. We are addicted people pleasers.

I have identified this addiction in myself, and every day as I get myself into situations where my addiction rears its head, I stop. I ask, "Is this a positive response or is it negative?" Because pleasing isn't always negative.

Once again we need balance. But any time we please, and it goes against our own true selves and identities, then we've gotten out of balance and we're struggling and wondering why we're so unhappy.

This struggle once again is the Me coming up and saying, "Look at my sacrifice," and then we're getting mad at others because they're not seeing our value. It will never work this way. We are wrong to expect them to see our value if we are not first seeing our own value. Isn't that right? When we value ourselves first, then others start to value us. And if you don't believe that, I'm here to tell you it is the truth. Don't live your life allowing others to dictate to you what your value is because it will be the biggest lie. We need to get quiet and ask: Who am I? What is my value? What do I like? What do I dislike?

Some of you have gotten so far off track that you don't know. But that's your first step, realizing you don't know and now going to the One who does know; our God. And don't be scared to start today. Some of you may be thinking, I don't want to know, because it may change my whole life. I can assure you it won't. Instead it will balance out your life and make it richer and fuller. Let's say that you love being a wife and mother, those things will not change. But if you allow yourself to speak, you may find that you love to garden and plant flowers. And if we seek out God in this, He will open a doorway for you to landscape your home, or to possibly get a part-time job working at a nursery. See these as small things that change your life for the better.

Then what happens is now because we're getting filled up with our own desires and dreams, we can become better and happier wives and mothers. Many times we are so scared of change that we never see the change as the very thing that will bring us true happiness and true worth. It is when our dreams and desires pass us by that we go on in life never being fulfilled and lying to ourselves that my husband should fill me, my children should fill me. And when they don't because they can't; then we're unhappy, blaming, and remaining.

Realize today that you have a choice to be happy or miserable. Many of you think, I don't have a choice. That is the biggest Me lie. We always have choices. But we have to seek out those choices. Form our plan. Trust in God to help us, and then wait for God's perfect timing.

Some of you will have so many choices you won't know which to pick. This is now a time of thought, reflection, and prayer because you don't want the enemy to get a victory here, because if you once again pick the wrong choice, you'll run your self weary doing, and not listening. God always has a perfect plan for us but if we don't go to Him and really listen, we can never find that perfect plan. And once we identify what that plan is, it will be God doing, God leading, and us following along like sheep, trusting in the Shepherd to guide and instruct. The Shepherd is not harsh. He doesn't take the staff and beat the sheep. He prods and pokes them in the right direction.

If it were up to the sheep to lead, they'd be lost, killed, or confused about where to go. God is not the author of confusion. That's the devil's scheme. The devil works overtime to deceive us into believing that it's our fault, or somebody else's fault, and tells us that we will never know our true path. But praise God, He always leads us back. He looks and longs to find you and bring you back.

> And therefore the Lord [earnestly] waits [expecting, looking, and longing] to be gracious to you; and therefore He lifts Himself up, that He may have mercy on you and show loving-kindness to you. For the Lord is a God of justice. Blessed (happy, fortunate, to be envied) are all those who earnestly wait for Him, who expect and look and long for Him [for His victory, His favor, His love, His peace, His joy, and His matchless, unbroken companionship]!
>
> Isaiah 30:18 (Amplified Bible)

And once we're back in the fold, then all things can unfold for us as was His previous desire all along. So will you choose today to seek, to discover, and to really listen to yourself and to God? And don't expect overnight success. God longs for us to seek Him, and God may even hide from you because He wants you to seek Him in determination and with an unfailing spirit. He knows what it's going to take for you to get your dreams and desires, and if you can't today have the will to stick with something, then tomorrow when you need that same discipline, you will also give up. See, we're back to discipline.

Let's take the example of a dirty house. Many of us have dirty homes. Dishes are in the sink piling up, laundry is on the floor, and dust is everywhere. We all long to have clean homes. But if we don't have the discipline to get up and tackle the mess, the mess will not go away. I'm just as much to blame as you are. At one time I was having a small pity party, and I went for weeks not cleaning my kitchen. I'd clean the rest of my house, but the kitchen was a disaster. I kept telling myself, "When I run out of counter room I'll clean the kitchen." But of course I always kept on finding more room. I even had things on the floor. And I really got this, "I don't care attitude." But eventually I did get sick of it, and the Spirit of God just came to me very gently and said, "If you would just start the small discipline of taking fifteen minutes to do the work, then your kitchen would always be clean." So I listened. I took the pressure off myself, and now I do have that discipline, and a clean kitchen. And you can have this also.

So take the pressure off yourself, see what small steps you can start today, and don't look back. This is all determination. Determination is just another word for discipline. But we lose our determination because we get too harsh with ourselves. Don't allow the "I don't care attitude" to dictate. This causes us misery. So many people live a miserable life because of this failing attitude, and the enemy loves it. Don't let the enemy win. We are the winners, but a winner has to first get in the race. If we never even get in the race, how can we ever win anything?

God today is standing there with your entry papers, will you take them? Will you believe in something beyond yourself? Some of us are so hurt and wounded that it's so hard to believe. But guess what? God believes for you, and if you take that first step, then that belief will jump on you. So go for it! Believe today, ask God to believe for you, and you act. It's all about us acting. You can do it, this action is your first step to belief and then see what amazing things God will do for you.

> And Jesus said… [You say to me]. If you can do anything? [Why] all things can be (are possible) to him who believes!
>
> At once the father of the boy gave [an eager, piercing, inarticulate] cry with tears, and he said, "Lord, I believe! [Constantly] help my weakness of faith!"
>
> Mark 9:23–24 (Amplified Bible)

What did he ask for? He asked for God, even in his unbelief, to bless him. He didn't have to wait until he was whole and complete in his belief; he pushed straight ahead in his own weak unbelief, and still got his blessing. And so can you.

The enemy lies to us and says you can't ask for anything until you have this problem worked out, or this amount of faith, or this, or this. These are lies. God longs to bless you. He waits to bless you. What is stopping Him? It is us. Be bold and fervent today; truckloads of blessings are waiting for you. What does it take? An asking heart, a willing and obedient spirit and an accepting attitude. "Go for Gold," and gold shall be given to you.

CHAPTER V

I thought I knew it all
I didn't
I thought I could do it all
I couldn't
I thought I was smart enough
I wasn't
I thought I was brave enough
I was weak
I thought,
I thought,
I thought.

Our thoughts can really get us into trouble. We think we know, but we don't know. It's only with time and experience that we learn. It's all about learning. So many times we even say, "I think," but what we need to say is, "What have I learned?"

The old Me beliefs will come in, and if we don't question them, they will rule our lives. But if we would stop and ask, "What have I learned and what should I be doing in this situation?" then we can have real clarity and decisiveness about what we need to do. But too many times we are lazy about asking ourselves and we fall into traps and say to ourselves later, "Why is my life in such a mess?"

It is an act of will to bring up our knowledge. But as we bring it up and then bring it up again, then it will become a habit. And when we fall into repeating situations that same knowledge will automatically come up to warn and instruct us.

We have to be determined to listen. We can have so much knowledge about ourselves and our behaviors but if we never use that knowledge, then it can never help us. Nobody likes falling into a repeated rut. And the reason why we do is because we don't listen. We don't face the hard questions about our self and we don't stop ourselves. We have this Me belief, this time it will work out all right. Wrong! How can it? It's a rut. What happens when you get into a rut? You get stuck and you just keep on repeating the same cycle.

What happened to Winnie the Pooh? He and his friends we're all looking for home, but they kept on finding the same pit. So Winnie said, "Maybe if we look for the pit, we'll find home." And they did! We all need to look for our own pitfalls. If we don't see the pitfalls and the traps, then we'll just keep on landing in them. We all know that we need to learn from our mistakes. And many of us are gaining ground, in this area. But if we're not extremely careful the Me will fool you and tell you this situation is totally different than the last. And in the end you'll discover it was the exact same trap.

And where is God in all this? He's there, as the shepherd trying to lead us. But the Me belief in us is so dominant that many times it will shut out other voices of reason. We have to actively seek to hear those voices of reason, we have to identify and ask is this "kind of" the same thing? It may not be the exact same thing, but if you can say kind of, you better start running. And when the Me tells you it will work out, run harder. But it has to be an act of our own will. If we are not willing to change we will never change.

The Me will continue to control us no matter how mad we get. No matter how many books we read about our problems, or how much we cry and call out to God, we will never gain complete and total victory because once again we're not doing, we're thinking, and the Me loves it.

I have come to the point in my life where I'm afraid to think. So daily I tell God, "I don't know. I don't know. I don't know, but I know You know, and that's good enough for me."

See what I'm doing? I'm trusting God. I'm not testing God. It's disobedience that tests God, but it's obedience that trusts God. When we test God we are not trusting. One way that I totally trust God is in my finances, I let Him lead me, to be a good steward, and to know the difference between my needs and my wants, because we can want a whole lot but not necessarily need any of it.

> And they who know Your name [who have experience and acquaintance with Your mercy] will lean on and confidently put their trust in You, for You, Lord, have not forsaken those who seek (inquire of and for) You [on authority of God's Word and the right of their necessity].
>
> Psalms 9:10 (Amplified Bible)

God is not offended when we give it all to Him. The spirit in us rises up to do the work because now God can come in and totally change and renew us. Our problem is we are too full of ourselves. God has to try and test us so we will run out of our own know-how and totally depend on God's know-how. Why does He say, "Come as little children"? A child doesn't question; a child just does. When we put it in God's hand the Me is weakened. But even a weak Me can still get us into a lot of trouble.

So then we always have to come back to, "What have I learned? What do I know?"

What does it look like? Even though we have turned the knowing over to God, we still live, act, and think, but now we have to live, act, and think decisively. We have to keep up our guard in these beginning stages because if we don't and fall into the pit, then we're right back where we started.

Here's an example: you quit smoking, and you're getting a lot of victory, and you feel good. But the lying Me comes in and says, "You can still sit and hang out with your smoking friends." Wrong. Why? because if you're around and in association with that behavior, it will jump right back on you. But if you question the Me and say, "They're still my friends, and I'll only hang out with them in a smoke-free environment. Then our resolve to quit gets stronger, and we haven't lost our friends. A perfect example is at work. Many businesses are smoke free. Be in association with your friends in the building, but don't be in association in the smoking area because that very same behavior will come back on you and you'll have lost all your victory. Then you'll be down the same road—miserable, trying to quit again. And many people do this their entire lives, never realizing that they have the knowledge and learning to kick the habit. It's once again us identifying the traps and not falling into them. Don't live your life falling into one trap after another.

We see people every day who have allowed themselves to time after time get free, and then lose it, get free again, and then lose it again. And you look at them and they're just tired and worn out, never realizing why. Because they put on blinders and walked with no sense of direction and wham, they've fallen once again into the same trap. The sad truth is, eventually they give up and live this down, depressed, purposeless life, never knowing why. And they will affirm until the day they die how hard they worked, how hard they struggled, how they tried everything and it was impossible. It's not impossible. It's hard, but God is always leading and guiding us, but we have to listen. Too many times it's us once again thinking and not depending on God.

> For no temptation (no trial regarded as enticing to sin, no matter how it comes or where it leads) has overtaken you and laid hold on you that is not common to man [that is, no temptation or trial has come to you that is beyond human resistance and that is not adjusted and adapted and belonging to human experience, and such as man can bear]. But God is faithful [to His Word and to His compassionate nature], and He [can be trusted] not to let you be tempted and tried and assayed beyond your ability and strength of resistance and power to endure, but with the temptation He will [always] also provide the way out (the means of escape to a landing place), that you may be capable and strong and powerful to bear up under it patiently.
>
> 1 Corinthians 10:12 (Amplified Bible)

If we never see those resting places along the road, and don't seek their refuge, then we can never get free. It is when we are weakest that we lose the battle. Seek out those places of rest, shelter, and refreshment. And then, once again enter the battle, but this time being much more wiser and stronger, and I guarantee you will win.

Let's go back to the smoker. One place of shelter is in our own homes. For many, they are the only ones in the household who smoke. Sometimes you'll even hear people say, "I never smoke at home." This is a great start. Continue in that behavior. Ask for encouragement from family and friends and then expand that area toward work. There are only twenty-four hours in a day. Eight hours we're sleeping, eight we're at home, and eight we're working. So really the only place we have to smoke is in the car and at work. And then we can start working on those times.

Take things in chunks. We kill ourselves, by trying to carry the whole load. Do what you can do, and then let God do the rest. Remember, casting our cares but not our responsibility. And don't be thinking we're picking on the smokers, we love the smokers. But we all want to get better. Once again see this as an example.

So let's start today. Get excited about this new direction in your life! Go at it strong, and when you get weak, seek renewal, and then go at it again; and if you fail? One of the saddest things about failure is people don't realize that it's human to fail. We are human. But just because you fail doesn't mean it's over. It was just a minor setback. But study after study has proven if you try again, and you try again, and again and again, and you don't stop you will get the victory. You are on the victory road today, and your victory is in front of you. But if you get off the road then you can never succeed. Don't get off the road. Don't quit, just keep on keeping on. God's here for you. He will never leave you or forsake you. He's your coach. He's cheering you on.

CHAPTER IV

Don't spend your whole life on the wrong path.
Ask today what your path is, and keep
on asking until you get an answer. We're
never too old, we're never too young, never
too uneducated, never too anything, to
get back on track and find our destiny.

Another way to find our true destiny is to identify with who we are. So many of us have lost our identity, we really don't know who we are. Oh we think we know, but we can think a whole lot and in the end be dead wrong. We need to back up, get quiet, and start asking, seeking, and contemplating who we are.

Part of our problem is, we never think to ask. We take it for granted we know. But really in life we don't know. If we did we would be happy in our lives, fulfilled and on our way. But we're not. Oh some rare ones are, because they've taken the steps and done the work to find out.

Please seek today to find out. Get quiet. Get alone. Have the discipline to find out. It will change your life, and set you on the path to happiness and fulfillment. Isn't that what you want? So why aren't we doing it? Because we haven't thought to do it. We think what we're doing will eventually make us happy. Sorry! Wrong! If it hasn't made you happy today, how can it ever make you happy tomorrow? It's once again our Me belief that is wrong. So what are our steps?

Discover your destiny. Identify with who you are. Seek to cultivate your worth. How do we do this? One way is we pray. Seeking God's guidance in our lives is very important, God is not afraid to show us the way, it is up to us to seek out His wisdom.

Depending on how you were raised, your self-worth in inwrought, it is a part of our inner identity. If our identity is dysfunctional then it is up to us to change our self-image and the only healthy way we can do that is to seek out God, and the word. For myself I looked at the men and women of the bible and tried to see myself in their struggles and to see how God worked through them to give them a glorious future, you can do this also. God will help you and give you a plan of action, trust Him and He will lead you.

If you work today to start implementing these steps, you will be on your way to finding happiness and true fulfillment in your life. Roadblocks will come up. It won't be easy. Many times it will be hard. But if you are tenacious and don't give up, you will get everything you have ever dreamed of and so much more.

Our God is so wonderful. He likes to surprise us with the wonder of His gifts and blessings. With God many times He will cause us to turn a corner, and when that happens go with it, because it's God leading us down the better path. At this time don't be thinking, just get in the habit of doing. And in the end God will make it work out better than we could ever dream.

See God. He is bigger and wider than we can ever be. We as man will always pick the inferior, God as God picks the highest and best. Because of our humanness, our lack of worth comes in and we say, "Oh I could never have that." But God desires to give to those who will seek Him.

> I love those who love me, and those who seek me early and diligently shall find me. Riches and honor are with me…
>
> Proverbs 8:17–18 (Amplified Bible)

If you're trying to seek your own riches and honor, you're going to fall flat on your face, or you'll have to compromise yourself so much that you can never truly be happy. We all know many rich people who have no true happiness.

But good news, there's hope for us all. God gives us that hope, and then He directs us and guides us into the path of truth. Don't be afraid of truth. This is where the enemy can steal from us if we're not careful.

How? Many of us are runners, always running from our own blame and responsibility. I'm a runner also. We run from the fault, and say it's their fault. We run from bad mistakes and choices, and say, "If I'd only known." We run from forgiveness and fall into bitterness and resentment. The truth exposes us. And we will never stop running until we are ready to face ourselves, our mistakes, our un-forgiveness, and our wrong me beliefs. And is it easy? No! It's hard, it's exposing, and it's looking at yourself and getting real. Until we decide to get real with ourselves, we can never get free and be on the path of self-discovery and true happiness.

And once again we're back to discipline. We all have discipline. It takes discipline to go to work every day. It takes discipline to clean our houses and take care of our families. I'm not asking you to do anything you haven't already been doing, and doing for years. I'm asking you now to focus in on yourself, and engineer that discipline in key areas that will open your world and make it so much richer and fuller than it has ever been before. If we're not seeking we're dying. Most of us are dying. I was dying for years. No, I didn't have any ailments, no diseases, but I had no life either. I just existed.

God instills in us that desire and dream to seek for something better. He will even put people in our path who have something; we don't know what it is, but man we sure want it. It's the life of God. It's that indwelling spirit that picks us up and instills in us life. That's not to say you'll never have any problems, but now when problems do come up, we have new life and energy to tackle them and they don't weigh us down as before. What we have is God. We have something the world can never give us. Our spouse can't and our jobs can't,because for many of us those are our problems. So cheer up. God is here.

> I have told you these things, so that in Me you may have [perfect] peace and confidence. In the world you have tribulation and trials and distress and frustration; but be of good cheer [take courage; be confident, certain, undaunted]! For I have overcome the world. [I have deprived it of power to harm you and have conquered it for you.]
>
> John 16:33 (Amplified Bible)

It's not about us doing it. It's all about God doing it. I could quote hundreds of scriptures, and they would all tell you the same thing. Let God be God. God wants you to have victory; He wants you to have joy, happiness, prosperity. We block ourselves. How? Disobedience is number one. We're on the path, but we're either ahead of God, or behind not doing what He said. Or we give up. I'm telling you it's going to be hard, but don't let go of God's hand. For many of us, just knowing something is hard we set our minds to expect it to be hard. Too many times we haven't been told how hard something is and we get in it and "lose it" because we set ourselves up for an easier road.

There is a mountain in Africa where the summit is attainable by walking the mountain path. And at different times of the year the sun is shining and you can reach the summit in leisurely fashion. But if you go another time of year, it's raining and slippery and hard to walk the same mountain path. Either way you can still reach the summit, but now with more effort and determination than ever before. And those who make it receive the high of having accomplished a great feat. God makes things hard sometimes because He knows what we don't; what it's going to take to get you to your destiny.

All roads are different. Don't look at someone else and say, "Well they had it easier." Look at yourself because only your destiny is for you. The devil loves to run us by people who have gotten the same thing easier than we did. And we get off track.

We let go of God's hand, and then God has to work to get us back on track. You need to stay on track. Set your mind and keep it set. And when you fail, get up, get determined, and get moving. We have to get stubborn with ourselves. We can't allow the Me to come in and deter us, because it will. So get disciplined, put the Me in its place, and keep putting it there until it settles down. And it will, but just as a small child has to be told again and again so does the Me. Remember the Me can never make us happy. Only the Self can. Let the Self work for you today.

Embrace discipline, and don't look back. Who in the Bible looked back? Remember Lot's wife? We had a party one time at my church where name tags were put on our backs, which we could not see. And the game was to ask others questions, and guess from their answers who you were. Guess what my name was? Lot's wife. For those who don't know who Lot's wife was, she was turned into a pillar of salt because of her disobedience of looking back at the destroyed city of Sodom (Genesis 19:26). God used that in me to teach me about this principal of always looking at others and looking back when He wanted me to go forward. But praise

God I never let go of His hand. If I would have used knowledge, I could have saved myself real heartache and misery.

Have you ever seen a child walking, and the adult is leading but the child is looking every which way and not looking ahead, and Wham! They walk into the wall. That was me! But if you watch them they're not really hurt, just startled. Watch out for the wall. Look ahead and hold on tight to the One who knows where to go.

CHAPTER VII

If you seek after truth
Happiness will find you

That is a promise from our wonderful God. Once again, it doesn't happen overnight, but praise God you're now on your way. All you have to do is keep on going forward. What do you have to lose? What you tried before didn't work. So go in a new direction. Start today and don't look back. Keep looking forward, keep seeking and trusting in God for He knows the path even when it seems like we're lost and confused.

It's always God wanting us to get closer to Him. When we walk down a road and we don't know where we're going, we stick close to our companion because we know they know the way. They've gone this road before.

But any time we turn away from them, it's a sure thing that we're going to get lost because we don't know the path. So don't lose your companion. Stick to Him closer than a brother, especially when it gets dark because I can assure you it will. Or when it's raining and cold, stick close to Him for warmth and comfort because He'll lead you to the shelters along the way. He'll lead you to the food supply, and He'll lead you to your destiny. When we seek God as our guide, we totally put our life into God's hands. We don't argue when He says, "Go this way." We just do it because we trust that He knows. That's why we hired Him. Because He has the experience, He has the maps, He has the knowledge. So start today on your adventure and trust the guide completely.

So now we're progressing. We have picked our guide and we're following the path. But what is the most important thing? We need to listen to the guide. Remember that was our first discipline? Why? Because we can't successfully follow the guide if we don't listen. This trip isn't a sole venture. It's a partnership. If we're not willing to listen, then the guide can't help us. Knowing the Me, the guide will direct and our minds say, "Wrong, what you're telling me to do is crazy." Have you ever gotten one of those demands? And we look at the guide like they have three heads. Remember, they have been this way before. We haven't. This is all new to us. We have no experience, we have no knowledge. We have past experience, but how many of you know that what we think will work in this new situation doesn't work at all? And then we're standing there saying, "Well, I thought..." Did you forget? We're not supposed to be thinking, we're supposed to be doing.

Does this mean we're never supposed to think for ourselves at all? No, of course not. As you're traveling you'll pick up knowledge, and we always have our former knowledge.

If the guide says to build a fire. We have knowledge to build the fire. But we get in trouble when we come to the forks in the road. We know how to identify a fork in the road, we know what it looks like, and if you've been with the guide for any duration of time He's there telling you. That's when we cast aside our own thoughts and go with the guide's. That's why He's called the guide, because He's guiding. We're not guiding. If it we're up to us, we'd be lost, starving, and in peril for our lives

We have to trust. For some of us that's very hard. We are independent people who have gone through most of our life doing for ourselves, and most of the time it's worked out. But now we have to realize we're treading on new ground. We're seeking after something higher and wider than we could ever envision.

Let's take the example of a building. Many of us can build some kind of shelter. Some of our shelters will be a lean-to, others a log cabin, and even others a well-built home. If we're trying to build a fifty-story building, we're going to have a disaster on our hands if we don't put aside our own independence and seek out those with more knowledge and engineering. In building a fifty-story building we need a team of experts, not our own knowledge because it is inferior. We need to apply this same principal to our own lives.

If you want to live your same-old-same-old life, then the knowledge you have will build you the shelter. But if we want to reach out for the higher and wider dream or vision, we have to put aside the Me and walk forward trusting in the builder and following Him. And you will be amazed at the building you will create.

> Except the Lord builds the house, they labor in vain who build it…
>
> Psalm 127:1 (Amplified Bible)

We labor in vain, why? Because we cannot achieve true greatness without the master builder. He is the master, not us. Remember, we're always thinking too much and overly relying on the Me. The master depends on His knowledge. We don't have this knowledge. We haven't built any high-rise buildings. The master has built hundreds. We need to totally lean on Him. To lean means to trust, rely, and believe in Him. This is an action of our belief. So many people say, "I believe, I believe," but they haven't any action behind that belief. It's thinking, but not doing. If we're not doing, then how can the building ever be built? We can think until the day we die, and never do anything. Now does that mean everything you try will work out? No, but at least you're trying and doing.

This brings in our hope. If I keep on doing, if I keep on trying, eventually something has to work. But if you sit and do nothing, nothing will work. And that is a sad legacy, but a legacy many of us get. What stops us from doing? Fear of failure. But if you never try, you have failed already. Don't live your life in fear. Reach out and try today.

Many of you are saying, "How? How do you get beyond the fear and the doubt?" I have a trick I use. I ask myself, "What is the worst that can happen?" And I make myself visualize the worst. And you know what happens? I discover the worst isn't all that bad. It is really our fear of the unknown that paralyzes us. And because of that unknown we don't act. We need to push beyond that, and if it doesn't work, then we walk away with knowledge. When we walk away with knowledge we never lose, we only gain.

We only lose when we gain no knowledge, and continue to live our lives in a demoralized and frightened atmosphere. When we gain knowledge, we actually gain true worth of ourselves. We are people who have been told not to push. We need not to push others, but we vitally need to push ourselves. It is in the struggle that we grow wiser and stronger. It all has to come back to the Self.

The Me has come in and wants to do this pushy behavior on others, but we need to put aside the Me and use this behavior towards the Self. Then the Self can emerge. The Self will never emerge without struggle. It has to struggle to push out the Me. The Me for many of us dominates our lives, and has maintained that dominance by force. Only a greater force will cast it out. Remember the Self is quiet, but the Self will exert itself as we allow it to emerge. And as it emerges it will get stronger and stronger, and it will become a force of change, renewal, and awaking in our lives.

The Me can only lie to us and give us a false sense of ourselves. It is not a true sense of who we really are. That only comes with the emergence of the Self. All our lives we have been told, "Do this, do that." I believed for thirty years if I only had more money, I would truly be happy. It was the biggest lie, because I got money and was miserable. And I said, "God, I'm supposed to be happy. What's wrong?" I had been seeking an outward happiness, outside of the Self, and it didn't work. Find your self and then all these other things shall be added unto you. Why? Because the Self always leads us back to God. The Self is really our inner spirit that leads and guides us to the truth.

> And you will know the Truth, and the Truth will set you free.
>
> John 8:32 (Amplified Bible)

What is this freeing? It's the Self.

It's a seeking, a striving, and a battle to get to that inner knowing of who we really are. Today seek to engage this battle. You are not alone. God is here. He's directing and guiding. Follow Him. Don't turn to the right or to the left, but walk forward. We have so much to gain and nothing to lose. All we lose is this dominance of the Me. The Me will still be there. It has to be. It needs to get us up in the morning. But now it will come into a balance with the Self. The Self will emerge. It will teach and instruct towards the truth, and will then give us the happiness we all so desperately strive for. It won't be an empty bag, but a beautiful birth of our spirit that connects us to God. Don't allow the Me to disconnect you from yourself or from God. Don't continue another day. Knowledge is here for you. It beckons and yearns for you to receive of its bounty. But it won't push you or force you, you have to embrace it. And oh what glories of glories it will bestow upon you.

> Your [infinite] knowledge is too wonderful for ME, it is high above ME, I cannot reach it.
>
> Psalm 139:6 (Amplified Bible)

Did you see it? The Me can never satisfy. It is only the Self, and the Self brings us back to God.

> And in [exercising] knowledge [develop] self-control and in [exercising] self-control [develop] steadfastness (patience, endurance), and in [exercising] steadfastness [develop] godliness (piety).
>
> 2 Peter 1:6 (Amplified Bible)

God unfolds His infinite knowledge only to the Self. Why? Because the Self walks in humility and the Me walks in pride. When we humble ourselves and we believe as an action, God comes closer to us and He changes our world. Let Him change your world today. We all want our world to be changed. Some of you are screaming and begging for that change. Don't delay another minute.

Take these steps and walk into His glorious light. Because that's what it is. The light shines all around us and we can see. The light is wonderful, but it can also expose us. But whenever we're walking in truth, we always need that exposure. Don't be afraid of the truth, the truth will lead you to yourself. Yes, the truth hurts. But just like a broken bone, as it's healing it doesn't always feel the greatest, but it's healing and so are we. Some of us are so wounded, and our Me beliefs lie to us and tell us, "It's not our fault, it's their fault." More times than not, that's just not true. It's us repeating the same cycle. And until we expose our behavior and see our own faults we will never break out of that cycle. Don't let the Me cycle continue another day.

I'll give you an example about me, exposing myself. I kept having this same cycle when it came to men. I was chaste. The road to chastity is not an easy road, but it is a rewarding road. And if you fall off it, you just have to work to get back on it. We can be in relationships with men and still be chaste. I always saw their faults, but never my own. Finally I started crying out to God and He got a great book into my hands. It exposed me. It showed me. It identified me. And it wasn't a pretty picture. But if I never had allowed myself to be exposed I'd still be blaming, never healing and going on to true victory, and increasing the worth in myself. It was so hard to see myself and my faults. But, "Oh, Praise

God," I've gained the knowledge. I woke up the next morning and I said,

"Today is my independence day."

You can have an independence day too. Don't you want it? God wants to give it to you. Don't be afraid. There's only glory, and joy, and awakening when you go down this path. And there are tears, lots of tears, but that's our healing. I don't know about you, but I've got holes inside of me. Only exposing myself and not hiding or running, but totally leaning on God, has healed me. And I've got a ways to go, but every day I'm on the path and I'm getting healed and getting stronger.

We have a desire planted in us, a desire to always be striving for the best, a desire to want more, to have more. But it only comes by going down the path of self-discovery. If we're not on the path, what are we doing? We're living the same-old life of misery.

The world will lie to you. The Me will lie to you. The devil will lie to you. And if we're not extremely careful we'll start believing those lies, and walking in those lies. What are those lies? "You can't do anything." "Nothing's going to change." "It's forever going to be this way."

Don't Believe the Me lies. Shake them off today and walk in the belief that things will change. All you have to do is look at the weather, to know that lie is wrong. Things change every single day. Others have succeeded, why can't you? Believe it, and it will happen for you. Not overnight. Remember it's a birthing and a growing. And even if you're a slow grower, you're still growing. Before you weren't growing at all, you were sitting there doing nothing. Now you're doing something. And give yourself time. Sometimes I will say, "God if this takes twenty years I'm doing it, I won't stop and I will succeed." By God's grace we have the twenty years to live anyway. Now most times it won't take that long, but praise God if it does. He gives us the grace. But I'm using this as an example so that you'll take the pressure off yourself. Because I can assure you, the Me will come in, the devil will come in, and the world will come in and say this isn't working at all. And you can say, "I don't see anything, I don't feel anything, but I believe." God's word is true. God promises us in the Bible, time after time, that He is working and the desires in our heart will come to pass.

> Delight yourself also in the Lord, and He will give you the desires and secret petitions of your heart.
>
> Psalms 37:4 (Amplified Bible)

But, they have to be righteous desires. God's not going to give you something that's unrighteous or unholy. Look at the example of Abraham or Joseph (Genesis 12–50). These men went through all kinds of adversity, but they always went down the God path of self-discovery, and in the end they received more than they could ever have envisioned. They didn't leave God on the path and say, "I'm going my way; see ya, God." They stuck by God when they were lost, when they were in prison, when they were falsely accused. They knew it would be God and God alone who would get them out of the mess. And if we get into messes, sometimes it's because we're doing something wrong. Sometimes it'll be God refining us for that higher glory. Joseph was put in prison not of his own fault but so God could refine him. And when he came out, he was gold. He didn't fall into the traps that a glittering Egyptian world could lead him down. He stuck by God every step of the way. If you receive the discipline of God now, later you'll still have that discipline and you won't get in trouble and lose everything God's given you. Discipline. Discipline. Discipline. Don't forget about discipline.

> For the time being no discipline brings joy, but seems grievous and painful; but afterwards it yields a peaceable fruit of righteousness to those who have been trained by it[a harvest of fruit which consists in righteousness-in conformity to God's will in purpose, thought, and action, resulting in right living and right standing with God].
>
> Hebrews 12:11 (Amplified Bible)

CHAPTER VIII

Who is the Me?
What is this force that controls us?
Do for me
Take care of me
See me
Help me
Love me
The Me demands but is never fulfilled
It wants but can never achieve
It longs but can never get
It hungers but is never fed
The Me controls
The Me mistreats
The Me
Only thinks
Me
Me
Me

We can really be controlled by and get wrapped up in the Me if we're not careful. The Me is demanding. It is not quiet, is not controlled, is not disciplined. The Me controls us. The Me has its purpose, but many of us have allowed the Me to enter areas that now are crippling and not healing. The Me is pushy. It always wants its own way. It's very selfish, and won't listen. Because the Me knows everything, right? The Me expects, but is not willing to give. It's not, "Help me, and I'll help you." No, it's, "You help me first, and then we'll see." If the me has another agenda, then everything else takes a back seat.

The Me is very hard on relationships. The Me keeps a score card and weighs every action, but never weighs its own actions. Its own actions are always right, are always good, are always perfect. The Me can never do anything wrong, it's everyone else doing things wrong, and we're just the victim. "Poor me!" And the Me really is poor because it is so short sighted. The Me only has one side, the "Me Side." The Me will tell you how much it loves you and cares for you. But really the Me can only love and care for itself. The Me is a small child who is hungry, wanting, and needing. But praise God there is hope for the Me. It's the Self. The Self is balanced, the Self sees. The Self discerns, the Self weighs, the Self looks, and the Self asks the hard questions. The Self seeks to expose the Self, because the Self hungers for knowledge of Self, and Self-awareness. The Me runs from these things. The Me hides its true nature. The Me knows that, "Nobody understands Me." The Me can never make us happy, it makes us miserable. Only the Self satisfies. The Self gives us Self-control, Self-fulfillment, Self-consciousness, Selflessness. All these working in harmony give us the much-desired fulfillment that we seek. And once again it's discipline, Self-discipline.

It's us seeking to coax the Self out. The Self is shy and reserved, but with continued encouragement and exposure the Self emerges as a mighty force in our lives that gives us new meaning. The Me only has meaning for the Me. The Self not only has meaning for the Self, but for its world and for others. The Me doesn't care about anything else, it just cares about the Me. If you are living your life today with the Me totally in control, you have no harmony or balance in your life. The Self seeks balance, and it seeks to have balance with the Me. Once again we need the Me. But we cannot allow the Me to dominate. That's always the Self's job. If you allow the Self to come in and gain control and bring balance to the Me. You will find your life much happier, much more fulfilled, and much more rewarding. Why? Because we have tuned into ourselves and sought to find our true identity, we have embraced our world and we look to make our world better and those around us better.

The Me never seeks for betterment of others, it only seeks for betterment of the Me. When the Self comes in and gains control, it then works at healing in all areas. This is what makes us happy. Is it easy? No. It's Self-mastery over every facet of our lives. Does this Self-mastery happen overnight? No, it takes years, but with each new unfolding our lives become treasures of beauty. We have no idea what's inside of us. The Self knows, and if we give it reign, it will draw up treasure after treasure of its riches. What are these riches? They are the areas in our life that give us fulfillment. These are our creative dreams and desires. These are our intuition, our knowledge, our wisdom, and our learning. The Me only seeks the feel good desires, the instant gratification, the highs in life. It can become very addictive to maintain these highs.

But along with the highs come the lows and that's when the Me stays in bed all the time and won't get up off the couch. It will drag itself to work but then complain all day, put down others and hate their jobs. Many of us do complain and hate our jobs, but the Me takes it to the extreme. When we allow the Me to control and dictate our lives, our creative dreams and desires are pushed in a corner.

And we're once again in the attitude, "I'd love to, but I can't." We'll no, if you allow the Me to dictate you can't do anything.

If you talk to successful people, what do they say?

Time after time, "I got an attitude; I wasn't going to stop, no matter how they laughed, no matter how often I failed, I pushed through." And they stuck with the plan!

You have to be careful if not everyone agrees with you, or is cheering you on, or believes for you, not to be stopped cold. That's really what it is; you want others to believe with you. And it never works. They don't have the dreams, they don't have the vision. They can't believe for you. You have to believe for yourself. Did you hear me? For yourself. Only the Self can get you where you want and need to go. And the Self is inside you, nowhere else. Not at work, not at your parents, not in all your clubs. It's a knowing that you have, that you have to nourish. You have to feed it, you have to believe in it and let it grow little bit by little bit. What is it? It's a harvest.

You plant the seed, you water it, you weed it, and you wait for the growth and the harvest. First you plant the seed. The Self emerges and you have a dream. But that dream can lay dormant until you plant it. And how do we plant it? We start looking for ways to bring it to completion. We set up a plan. We gain knowledge, we seek, we cultivate and we pray and ask God for His guidance and strength. Do all dreams come to fulfillment? No, not all. Because some dreams are just the Me again saying, "I want, I want," but never asking, "Is it good for me?"

So let's say we have our dream, and we're taking the steps of identifying if it's right and good for us. Now we start slowly working to get that dream or vision of what we want. We believe and we believe and we believe. And does it take days, weeks, and months? Possibly. But for most it will take years.

The first years are us just believing. So do we do nothing? No. We wait, we listen, and we seek, and as things come up, go ahead and do them. But what does the seed grow in? It grows in the soil and the soil is our rich belief. The soil has minerals and chemical properties that give the seed life and the ability to germinate. If we first don't believe, the dream cannot grow. This growth is our belief. If we don't discipline ourselves to believe, and to believe again, then the first minor storm will blow us over and possibly kill us. God is not in the business of failure. He is in the growing business. If you stick with God things will grow. It is when we leave God and try and do it ourselves that we fail. Oh we may succeed, but it can never be the rich harvest that we long for, because God is our fertilizer. We don't have any fertilizer. All we first have is belief, and even that without God is limiting because we limit ourselves. So get with God. Allow Him to fertilize your belief. Then stand back and watch your garden grow.

> So neither he who plants is anything nor he who waters, but [only] God who makes it grow and become greater. He who plants and he who waters are equal (one aim, of the same importance and esteem), yet each shall receive his own reward (wages), according to his own labor. For we are fellow workmen (joint promoters, laborers together) with and for God; you are God's garden and vineyard and field under cultivation, [you are] God's building.
>
> 1 Corinthians, 3:7–9 (Amplified Bible)

Next you water the seed. You talk to yourself, you keep the dream alive. You tell yourself over and over and over again that, "I will succeed." When setbacks happen, a flood comes in, or an animal, and digs you up. You just say, "Well, I've got to get grounded again." And you do the hard work to keep the belief of the dream alive because no plant that is not firmly grounded will survive and reach maturity. What is that grounding? It is God once again coming in and fertilizing that belief, making it stronger and stronger so that plant can stand against any and all adversity. Because adversity and trials will come. You think the devil is going to keep that fresh, green, luscious garden alone? No, he seeks to destroy, to weaken, and to kill. But if you stick to God no foe can withstand Him. God is the miracle worker.

Many time I have thought a plant was dead, you could have called me the brown thumb, but when I forgot about a plant and let it sit, you know what happened? A new green leaf would shoot up from the soil, and I'd discover it was never really dead. I had to be careful now with that new growth. I had knowledge of what I had done wrong previously and now I was more gentle and patient with that same plant. So today know that your dream is not dead. Just like that brown plant, it needed to be left alone and have patience applied to it.

> A man went out to dream. And as he dreamed, some dreams fell by the roadside, and the friends came and trampled them under. Other dreams fell on rocky ground where they had not much soil, and at once they sprang up, because they had no depth of soil. But when persecutions arose, they were scorched, and because they had no root, they dried up and withered away. Other dreams fell among thorns and the thorns choked them out, Other dreams fell on good ground, and because its soil was deep and well watered, it yielded, some a hundred times, some sixty and some thirty times as much as was sown.
>
> Adaptation from Parable of the Sower.
>
> Matthew 13:3–8.

Don't live your life allowing others to dictate to you what your dreams will be. You dream it, you seek it, and you go to God and ask, "Is this a righteous dream or is this just the Me." And if you do that time after time God will lead you where you need to go. He's the only One who can. We are like the sheep getting lost. Will you allow God to be your shepherd today? To lead you to the oasis of your dreams? To lead you to the good ground? What does a sheep live for? Good pastures with grazing that's sweet, water that's fresh and clear. Relief from predators and the shepherd's guiding hand.

Sheep are simple animals. They don't get caught up in things. Or if they do, it's because they've lost the shepherd. Don't lose the Shepherd. For many of us our lives are hectic and stressful but if we allow ourselves to take the example of the sheep, and allow God to be in charge then we can cast our cares unto Him, just as the sheep do with the shepherd. Will you become a sheep today and walk forward with the Shepherd leading all the way? Go for your dreams and never look back.

CHAPTER IX

One day I discovered myself
She was shy and kind
Never a cross word did she utter.
She showed me her beauty and her riches,
A sight to behold, she led me in
paths I could not walk alone.
Never weary and tired did I
become for she held me close,
She talked to me and I drew of her wisdom;
When I faltered her strength was there for me
Everyday we became closer we shared,
We grew, we laughed and we cried
She is a part of me, and I will never let her go.
I have a knowing that this is right
All my dreams unfold for me
As I walk by her side.

The Self longs to be in communion with the Me. And the Me can only be fulfilled with the indwelling of the Self. It's really a marriage. It's bringing two forces together that alone are incomplete. For alone the Me is demanding, pushy, and arrogant. And the Self alone is shy, quiet, and reserved. But when you bring them together in harmony, then their identities merge and you have a new birth of awareness, knowledge, and intuition. That could never be gained, for each alone. It takes two. Then you have something that is forceful, dynamic and mature. It's not weak, sickly, and dying. It's growing and it's getting stronger every day. It's just like our seed. It's getting all the right ingredients together, to give the plant the life force to unfold.

When you look at a seed, you have no idea what it's going to look like when it's grown completely. You think a flower. But we don't know what color. What size. What beauty. We have no idea what we will end up with. Many of us plan for one thing and get something totally different. I tell you God knows, and it will be more beautiful than we could ever envision. Don't limit yourself and don't limit God.

And will God come through and prune that dream? You better believe it. Will He come in and dig it up and move it? Yes, and yes again. As we feel and think the worst? Don't be feeling and don't be thinking. God knows we need better light, fresher soil, and a better water source. We just think, "Well I'm comfortable here." Wrong. You're going to be dead pretty soon too. Or you won't reach the growth or maturity that you need in that spot. But this other spot will have the nutrients and proper chemicals that you will need to be all you can be. If we allow God to be the gardener and allow Him total control He will direct and guide, and I can assure you it won't all feel good. But it will be the best for you. Remember, it's the Me that feels and the Self that obeys. Start obeying today. All our disobedience in the past has made us miserable. Get on this new discipline of obedience, for it is the Self that leads us into all paths of obedience, because the Self walks in integrity.

> Woe to him who strives with his Maker!-a worthless piece of broken pottery among other pieces equally worthless [and yet presuming to strive with his Maker]! Shall the clay say to him who fashions it, what do you think you are making?
>
> Isaiah 45:9 (Amplified Bible)

We are that clay. We are that unfolding of God's handiwork. We should not be fighting against the process. We have to allow the process to happen to us. Does the process always feel good? No, but as in any process, it is the end result that we are waiting and longing to achieve. Stick with the process today. Allow God to mold and form you into that beautiful creation, a creation we can never accomplish without God working in us. And it does take work. But we are people who are not afraid of hard work, as long as we know we're going to get a reward out of it. We seek for that reward, but most of us fail because we don't know what steps to take to get our reward. If you will follow the steps of totally trusting and leaning on God, even when the Me wants to run, with time, effort, and with God's help, you will get that reward. And it will be more rewarding than we could ever have dreamed.

It's no longer us doing it. It's now God doing it for us. God can only give to us when we are willing to give up ourselves; our ways, our plans, our dreams. And God will test us to see which is more important, the dream or Him. He is the one giving us our dream. Remember, God has to always be first. Second can be our dream. But if we flip-flop them, then God will come in and redirect and prune off the deadness of the Me. Because that's what's happened, the Me has reared its ugly head again. And we have gotten out of balance. Until we get this right, God will not give us our complete dream.

Let's say that many of you do have your dream. But still, if you don't get this right, you won't receive the highest fulfillment of that dream and many things will slip through your hands. Why? Because God is blocking you. We never see it. The Me says, "It's their fault, if this wouldn't have happened," and we blame, and we blame, and we blame.

Never realizing it's really us and our disobedience and God's controlling. Don't flip-flop your dream over God. This is so frustrating and people don't see it. They walk along in disobedience and only get a fraction of their dream. I mean if you can get a hundred percent yield, I don't want sixty or thirty. And why do people miss it?

They never see their own disobedience, and the Me is there once again lying and deceiving. Even though you have your dream, you're still frustrated and miserable. Seek today to identify where you have gotten off track. Seek God. Because somehow you have let go of His hand, thinking God is right there, when really we took a wrong turn a while ago. Once again get quiet, get introspective, and start seeking God's face. God is faithful to bring His presence to you. That is what we need. His presence, before we always had our presence and that presence lied to us, manipulated us, and quit on us when we needed it the most. But praise God, His presence never quits, never fails, never deceives. His presence is always true, it is loving and kind, always directing.

> For you will not abandon me to Sheol (the place of the dead), neither will You suffer Your holy one...to see corruption. You will show me the path of life; in Your presence is fullness of joy, at Your right hand there are pleasures forevermore.
>
> Psalms 16:10–11 (Amplified Bible)

God will never abandon us to the deadness of the Me. He is always drawing us closer to Him and to His wonderful riches. He wants to bestow upon us His blessings. But He can't give us those riches until we give up the Me and walk in obedience to His word. We all have a knowing inside of us: our conscience. We know what is right, and what is wrong. We want to say, "I don't know," but once again that's the Me lying to us. Don't believe the Me lies! They will steal from you your dreams and desires, or make those same desires and dreams a plague in your life. Don't clutch the prize in your hand and have it turn to dust. Once again we must follow the steps of listening, seeking and studying, and letting God lead us towards our dreams and desires.

> Jacob said, Swear to me today [that you are selling it to me]; and he swore to Jacob and sold him his birth right. Then Jacob gave Esau bread and stew of lentils, and he ate and drank and rose up and went his way. Thus Esau scorned his birthright as beneath his notice.
>
> Genesis 25:33–34 (Amplified Bible)

How sad for this young man named Esau. He never even saw what it was he gave away. This young man walked in disobedience and disobedience robbed from him his very life. Even though later he wept bitter tears of regret, he could never walk in the fullness of his blessings and dreams that had been given to him. He still got blessed, but it was dust in his mouth because he had the knowledge of what could have been. Most of us don't get this knowledge. We just believe that what we have is good enough. Please take a lesson from this man's failure. God has so much for us. We are the ones limiting ourselves. Why do we limit ourselves?

Some of it is lack of knowledge, some lack of worth, and some lack of desire. God can only give to us if we are willing to stretch ourselves out beyond our own limits, let God come in, and set up new limits. When we have no knowledge, we have no idea of what we can have. What is available, and what God says, He will do through us. How do we acquire this knowledge? We seek God. We spend time talking and meditating with God. We seek out His word, so God can speak to us. We pray, we fast. And we listen. God can only give to us if we are first willing to give something up.

What do we have to give up? First is time. We have to be willing to make an investment of our time to spend it with God. Spending our time with God enables God to teach us and to instruct us in the direction He wants us to go. It has to be a habit. We have to habitually desire and seek to spend this time with God. We have to cultivate this time. We have to plan out this time and later build on this time. Remember, God is looking and longing to bless you but He will only do it if we are looking and longing to bless God with our time, our abilities and our desires to do something great for God. Yes, it is our dream, but we have to see it as an avenue where God gets the victory. We all know that if we build it ourselves we will get a type of building, but if we allow God, the master builder, to build, He will make it into an awesome building.

> According to the grace (the special endowment for my task) of God bestowed on me, like a skillful architect and master builder I laid [the] foundation, and now another [man] is building upon it. But let each [man] be careful how he builds upon it.
>
> 1 Corinthians 3:10 (Amplified Bible)

God is always looking for the open heart, the ready spirit, and willing hands to do the work. But it has to be God's work, because our work by itself will turn to dust. God's work turns to gold.

> Now to Him Who, by (in consequence of) the [action of His] power that is at work within us, is able to [carry out His purpose and] do superabundantly, far over and above all that we [dare] ask or think [infinitely beyond our highest prayers, desires, thoughts, hopes, or dreams].
>
> Ephesians 3:20 (Amplified Bible)

Today will you seek out God for that work of gold that will transform your life into a life of abundance, wealth, and joy above any joy that we could acquire ourselves? Don't seek to do the work alone. Only God can supply, only God can achieve, and only God can turn our visions and dreams into a treasure of gold that no human hands have made. It's God's hands molding and shaping us to our destiny and fulfillment in our lives. He's waiting for you to turn and lean on Him. Will you? Will you embrace your new life, and walk in His victory and happiness for you? What have you got to lose? Nothing! Always know that God takes nothing and makes it beautiful.

> In the beginning God (prepared, formed, fashioned, and) created the heavens and the earth. The earth was without form and an empty waste, and darkness was upon the face of the great deep.
>
> Genesis 1:1–2 (Amplified Bible)

God will take your broken and shattered dreams, and mold them and shape them into a workable vessel. But it's up to us to first believe that He can and then turn it over to Him to do the work, and for us to wait and see what will unfold. Will you trust in God to do the work? He is waiting for you. Kneel down now and ask. He is faithful to supply.

CHAPTER X

Dreams of gold I see unfold
Their rays and brilliance are such to behold
Their beauty is astounding
How can I describe, no mere words can testify
For it is a creation That God has foretold,
He has planned it, He has envisioned it,
My limited thought could never have seen
What He has planned for me
When I look now at all I see, I see
the Master's hand in front of me,
He leads and guides,
He is stronger than Me, and
I know through it all
He takes care of me.

So now we are all thinking about that lost dream. With God on our side nothing's impossible. It's the devil's lies that we have believed, that have gotten us off track. It's not God. He is the one waiting for you to lift your burdens up to Him. Remember, with man it is impossible, but with God nothing is impossible. Why? Because we are so weak; we quit. We lay it aside. God is always building. God is always creating. And you can be assured with God, He will never finish until His work is done. But the sad truth for us is that if God can't complete the work in us He will find someone whom He can complete the work in.

The good news is, we now have knowledge on our side. God has come in once again, and given you a much-needed burst of energy. Take that energy and revive yourself, and revive your old cast aside dreams. It never went away; it has been laying there just waiting for you to pick it up. Now God is saying, "I'm with you, I won't leave you. This time we'll do it together."

It is always us leaving God; He never leaves us. But God will put you on a shelf. He has done this to me, and many times. But no matter how long I had to sit, I knew the master would come around and would move in my life to make that dream and vision complete. When we are sitting, it only means that other facets of the dream are now being worked out for its completion.

> For a dream comes with much business and painful effort, and a fool's voice with many words.
>
> Ecclesiastes 5:3 (Amplified Bible)

What does the fool do? He tries to do it on his own, spouting his own plans and desires, never leaning on God, and wonders why later he has such a mess. Don't get into a mess. A mess is just like being in the pit. But cheer up, God can even then get you out.

So what have we learned? Discipline in listening, discipline in waiting, and discipline in obedience. These are our key elements. These elements unlock our power to get our dreams and visions to come to pass. Always remember with time, as the vision unfolds, we're learning and seeking out the truth.

Your dream will take you up many hills and down many valleys. And the truth comes in when we realize that the dream is beyond us. It's a God thing. Its God leading, directing, and guiding, and us going along for the ride. So many times in my own life, God has taken a turn and the path became very scary and dark. But I always knew not to let go of the Master's hand and that He would lead me out. Remember, He's the guide. He has the maps. He knows the way, not us.

This path is really a path of sacrifice. It's not the Me

sacrificing to walk in pride, it is now the Self sacrificing to gain new knowledge and new direction. As we walk the unknown path to our destiny, we put aside our own ways and plans of doing things, and we walk in patience and lean not to our own understanding. We are leaning totally on the Guide's timing. Timing is key. No longer our time, but now a Godly time. There were so many things that I thought I should have right now. Praise God I never got them because the timing wasn't right. And I would have ended up in a mess.

We have identified the discipline that we need to walk this path. Next, we need to identify our destiny. You may have a dream and vision, but that doesn't necessarily mean that's your destiny. It's some of your destiny. Destiny encompasses more than just a single dream.

Look at a woman who has a dream to be a wife and mother. She dreams for this, she longs for this. And God gives her, her dream. But her destiny is not complete. She marries, she has children, she raises those children and then those children go on to have more children. Now she is not only a wife or a mother. Now she is a grandmother, and still later she'll become a great-grandmother. Her destiny has unfolded to birth a legacy that her dream first started but only her destiny could complete.

We need to look beyond our limited thinking to see God's plan and His desires for our lives. We can't do it alone; we have to do it with the destiny creator. And that's God. We serve an awesome God who longs to be "Big" in our life. Who longs to do "Big" things; things we could never even dream of because we don't think big enough. We think small. We think limited, but not God. All we have to do is look around and see how "Big" God thinks.

God is seeking today for you! For you to encompass a destiny and not just a dream.

We need the dream first, but knowing God, He will test us in that dream, and possibly even take the dream away so that now we can see beyond ourselves and really see God. Our eyes will fool us and lead us astray. If we lean on God, He will complete His work in us. My own dream has taken me so many places, but it has always been for my own growth. My growth as a person, but also as a child of God. God seeks for that growth in us; for that maturity. We need that maturity so the destiny can unfold.

Our destiny has to be built on a foundation of obedience to God. And when we have that obedience, we have humility. We are submissive to God. We humble ourselves by doing things His way, by walking in His statues, and His dictates. If we do this, then we have really allowed the Self to emerge. No longer does the Me control us, it is now a union of the Me and the Self, for the Self has acquired dominance and maturity, and a new attitude of spirit has replaced all our old disbeliefs and misconceptions.

> So then, we may no longer be children, tossed [like ships] to and fro between chance gusts of teaching and wavering with every changing wind of doctrine, [prey of] the cunning and cleverness of unscrupulous men, [gamblers engaged] in every shifting form of trickery in inventing errors to mislead. Rather, let our lives lovingly express truth [in all things, speaking truly]. Enfolded in love, let us grow up in every way and in all things into Him Who is the Head…
>
> Ephesians 4:14–15 (Amplified Bible)

God is seeking your maturity today. We all know maturity takes time. Don't fight the time. It will make you miserable, because it has made me. Now I have a lot of victory in this area, but misery has also followed me. Don't let it follow you. Gain the knowledge today that all things work in God's timing, not ours. In the meantime what are we to do? We need to live our lives. Every day we have responsibilities God expects us to keep, but now we have new life and new hope for a better life and a changing world; a world full of God's endless possibilities.

Continue to pray, to seek, to identify our limits, and to let God stretch us to see His limits. For many of you this is scary, this is new ground, but it's beautiful. The sun is shining, we're rising, and the view is unfolding before us. But always know that when the shadows of the day start to lengthen and the sun starts to fade that the Master hasn't left us, He's just waiting for a new birth of the sun. We will have the sun go up, the sun go down, and the sun go up again. But with each new cycle God is unfolding our destiny. We need to take the turns as they come. Never let go of the Master's hand and you will received all and more than you could ever fathom.

CHAPTER XI

The Beach
They walked hand in hand
He saw out of the corner of his eye
The headlights
Another car passing by
Going somewhere unknown
How he wishes he could go
But the cares of the world bind him down
He can remember when he was
young and free without a care,
But that seems so long ago.
And so he looks down the beach never divert-
ing and living a life that seems planned
But not his plan

Don't let this happen to your life. This man lost his path. He thought he had all he could ever dream of, but what he had lost was his Self. And because he had pushed it away, it had gotten quieter and quieter until now he's walking along the beach and the prick is there. He couldn't see God, he couldn't see his destiny. All he could see was his own dreams and the lie the world was feeding him. If today you feel that prick, harden not your heart for the prick is life trying to unfold. It's the green shoot of the plant. Don't smother it; give it light by the awakening of your thoughts. Give it water by the unleashing of your hope. Give it birth by the renewal of your spirit in God.

We need that Spirit of God to help us, to direct and to show us the path we must take to get our destiny. No path will ever be as fulfilling. No path will ever be as rewarding. No path will ever be as joyous. We fool ourselves in thinking another path can lead us to the same victory, and it never will, don't be afraid of hard work.

> The work of each [one] will become [plainly, open] known (shown for what it is); for the day…will disclose and declare it, because it will be revealed with fire, and the fire will test and critically appraise the character and worth of the work each person has done.
>
> If the work which any person has built on this Foundation [any product of his efforts whatever] survives [this test], he will get his reward.
>
> 1 Corinthians 3:13–14 (Amplified Bible)

And what is that Foundation? It is always God. Will you today start with God?

Will you open your heart, your mind, and your spirit to Him? He is the "Way Maker," no other way is before us except His way. Walk in this way and the way shall lead you home.

Never Give Up
Never Doubt
Never Forget
Never Stop
For Their Is A God
That Never Gives Up On Us
He Never Doubt Us
He Never Stops Us
We Stop Ourselves
We Turn Aside
We Lose The Dream
We Lose The Vision
Allow God
See God
Meet God
And God Will Turn Your Doubts
You're Fears
You're Limits
Inside-Out
It's His Work
Not Us Working Anymore.

Enter into the rest of God, for really that is what silence is all about. When we get silent it's because we've gotten beyond our Self. We've gotten weak. We've allowed that humble and submissive spirit to gain control. After we've raved, after we've cried until we can't cry anymore, the wonderful feeling of rest comes upon us and we rest from all our trying. Now the enemy will immediately come in and condemn you for what we misbelieve is our failure. If we turn aside from that condemnation and continue to rest, then the quiet Spirit of God will envelop us and we can have clarity and new direction for our lives. Never see this quietness as failure. Only now see it as the starting point to a new beginning.

Rest, rest in God, rest from your trying, rest from your seeking. And now let God come in and remold and reshape that perceived failure into the very thing that will lead you to your dreams, visions, and ultimate destiny. Go with God. Go with love and go with silence.